American Lives

Phillis Wheatley

Rick Burke

Heinemann Library
Chicago, Illinois

© 2003 Heinemann Library
a division of Reed Elsevier Inc.
Chicago, Illinois

Customer Service 888-454-2279

Visit our website at www.heinemannlibrary.com

Created by the publishing team
at Heinemann Library

Designed by Sarah Figlio
Photo Research by Dawn Friedman
Printed and Bound in the United States by
Lake Book Manufacturing, Inc.

07 06 05 04 03
10 9 8 7 6 5 4 3 2 1

Library of Congress Cataloging-in-Publication Data
Burke, Rick, 1957-
    Phillis Wheatley / Rick Burke.
      p. cm. — (American lives)
    Summary: Relates the story of a young girl
bought as a slave by a Boston family where she later
learned to write and became a poet.
    Includes bibliographical references and index.
    ISBN 1-4034-0730-4 (lib. bdg.) — ISBN 1-4034-3105-1 (pbk.)
    1. Wheatley, Phillis, 1753-1784—Juvenile literature. 2. Poets, American—Colonial
period, ca. 1600-1775—Biography—Juvenile literature. 3. African American women
poets—Biography—Juvenile literature. 4. Slaves—United States—Biography—Juvenile
literature. 5. African American poets—Biography—Juvenile literature.   [1. Wheatley,
Phillis, 1753-1784. 2. Poets, American. 3. Slaves. 4. African Americans—Biography.
5. Women—Biography.]   I. Title. II. Series: Burke, Rick, 1957-   . American lives.
    PS866.W5Z5826 2003
    811'.1—dc21
    [B]
                                          2002154418

Acknowledgments
The author and publishers are grateful to the
following for permission to reproduce copyright
material: Title page, p. 28 Schomburg Center for
Research in Black Culture/New York Public
Library; pp. 4, 5, 9, 12, 13T, 16, 22, 27 Bettmann/
Corbis; pp. 6, 25 Stock Montage, Inc.; p. 8
Courtesy of the Massachusetts Historical Society,
MHS image #4012; p. 10 Collection of the Mercer
Museum of the Bucks County Historical Society;
pp. 11, 20 Kevin Fleming/Corbis; pp. 13B, 21, 24
Hulton Archive/Getty Images; pp. 14, 15 North
Wind Picture Archives; p. 17 Courtesy of the
Massachusetts Historical Society, MHS image
#2168; p. 19 Historical Picture Archive/Corbis;
p. 23 Dave G. Houser/Corbis; p. 26 Richard
Cummins/Corbis; p. 29 copyright Elizabeth
Catlett/licensed by VAGA, New York, NY/
Cincinnati Art Museum

Cover photograph: Schomburg Center for
Research in Black Culture/New York Public Library

Special thanks to Patrick Halladay for his help in
the preparation of this book.

Every effort has been made to contact copyright
holders of any material reproduced in this book.
Any omissions will be rectified in subsequent
printings if notice is given to the publisher.

Some words are shown in bold, **like this.** You can
find out what they mean by looking in the glossary.

The cover of this book shows a portrait of African-American
poet Phillis Wheatley by an unknown artist.

Contents

Kidnapped .4

A New Land 6

The Wheatleys 8

Being Different 10

Poetry 12

Fame in Boston 14

A Published Poet 16

Great Britain and Freedom 18

Books, Sadness, and War 20

Meeting George Washington 22

Poor and Forgotten 24

Alone Again 26

An Amazing Woman 28

Glossary 30

More Books to Read 31

Places to Visit 31

Index 32

Kidnapped

The little girl is scared and sick. She is on a ship that is crossing the Atlantic Ocean. Even during the day, not much sunlight makes it down to the part of the ship where the little girl is. There are other people with her, but they are scared and sick, too.

Sometimes the ship is tossed from one large wave to another. That makes all the people with the little girl feel even sicker. Most of the people have never been on a ship before, and they have no idea where they are being taken.

The ships that slaves were taken to the colonies on were crowded and scary, as this 1860 drawing shows.

The little girl was stolen from her family. She was put in a small, dark room near the bottom of a ship with 75 other people. They are being taken to the American **colonies.** There, they will be sold as **slaves** and forced to work for other people for the rest of their lives. They will never see their families again, and most will never be free.

Phillis Wheatley is shown here as a teenager. This is what she probably looked like when she lived with the Wheatleys.

The little girl does become a slave, but she gains her freedom. She grows up. She learns how to read and write English. She becomes famous for her writing. The name that is given to her is Phillis Wheatley.

5

A New Land

The ship was named the *Phillis*. It arrived in the city of Boston in the **colony** of Massachusetts in the summer of 1761. **Slave** traders captured people in Africa and sold them as slaves in the American colonies. They made more money when they sold men, but most of the 75 Africans on the *Phillis* were women and children.

This painting shows a slave **auction**.

This upset Timothy Fitch, the man who owned the *Phillis*, because he wasn't going to make much money with this group of slaves. Plenty of people gathered along the docks on Boston's harbor for a chance to buy a person who would work for them.

The Life of Phillis Wheatley

1753	1761	1767	1773
Phillis's birthday is unknown, but some historians think it was in 1753.	Phillis was brought to Boston when she was about eight years old.	Phillis began writing poetry at about age fourteen.	Phillis visited London and her book is *published*.

The little girl walked off the ship wearing nothing but a piece of dirty rug that she had found on the ship. Fitch probably thought it wasn't going to be easy to sell her because she was very young, about seven or eight years old. She was also still sick from the long trip on the boat.

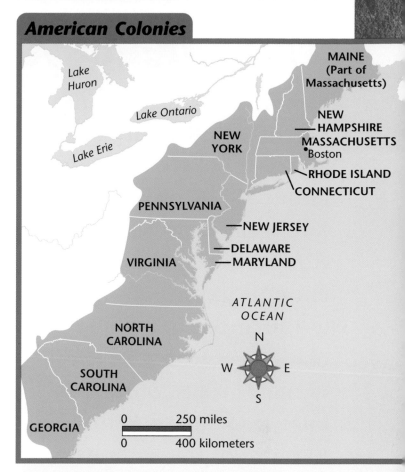

American Colonies

This map shows the colonies and where the city of Boston is located.

A woman named Susannah Wheatley bought the little girl. She named her Phillis, after the ship that brought the girl to Boston. The **carriage** ride to the Wheatleys' home began Phillis's new life in a new land.

1774	1776	1778	1784
Susannah Wheatley died on March 3.	*Phillis met George Washington in March.*	*Phillis married John Peters.*	*Died on December 5 in Boston.*

7

The Wheatleys

Susannah Wheatley and her husband, John, belonged to a wealthy family. They owned a large house on King Street in Boston. Susannah was rich enough to pick any **slave** at the **auction,** but she chose the sickly girl she named Phillis. Susannah later said she picked Phillis because of her interesting face and because of the way she stood. The Wheatleys quickly discovered that Phillis was smart.

A Street in Boston

King Street, which is called State Street today, was a busy street in Boston. Phillis saw many important events on King Street, such as the Boston Massacre, a fight in which five men were killed by British soldiers. Phillis wrote about some of these events in her poetry.

This drawing shows what King Street in Boston looked like in 1776.

Phillis learned how to speak English very quickly. The Wheatleys began to teach Phillis how to read and write. Mary, the Wheatleys' eighteen-year-old daughter, became Phillis's **tutor.**

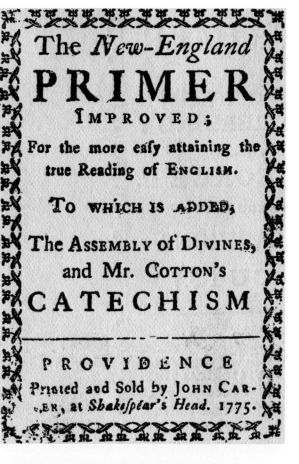

Teaching a slave how to read and write was against the law in some of the other **colonies.** There were more slaves in the southern American colonies than there

This is the cover of a book that was used in schools in the colonies to teach children how to read. It was printed in 1775.

were white people. Many white people there were afraid that the slaves would one day overpower and kill them. They believed that keeping the slaves uneducated helped white people stay in power and stay rich.

Being Different

In the Wheatley house, Phillis was treated differently than the Wheatleys' other **slaves** were. The Wheatleys didn't want Phillis to be friends with the other slaves in the house because they wanted Phillis to be more like a part of the family than a slave who served them. She had her own room, which had a table with a lamp so that she could read in her room at night.

While the other slaves had to work hard during the day and night, Phillis didn't have much to do. She would sometimes have to dust some furniture, but she didn't have to work as hard as the other slaves did.

This is a type of lamp that people in the **colonies** used. It had a wick like a candle's in the front, and it burned oil.

This is what the Old South Meeting House in Boston looks like today. Visitors can still see where the Wheatleys went to church.

Phillis's main job was keeping Susannah company. Susannah's children, Mary and her twin brother, Nathaniel, were both about to be married. Susannah was starting to feel lonely.

Phillis went to church with the Wheatley family every Sunday. They went to church at the Old South Meeting House in Boston. Slaves and black people were not allowed to sit with white people. The black people sat in another part of the church called the "African corner."

Poetry

Phillis spent large parts of her day reading the Bible and studying poetry. After a little more than a year in the Wheatley home, Phillis had learned to read and write English very well. She began to study Latin. Over the years she also studied history, **mythology, astronomy,** and **geography.** When Phillis was about fourteen years old, she began writing poetry. Poetry is a way for people to write about their thoughts and feelings.

This type of globe was used in Wheatley's time to study the stars, sun, and moon.

What Is Poetry?

Poetry is a form of writing that has rhythm, is usually short, and sometimes rhymes.

John Milton

Phillis enjoyed reading the writing of English poet John Milton. One of her favorite books was Milton's book Paradise Lost.

Susannah loved that Phillis was writing poetry. Phillis would stay up late at night writing at her table with the lamp in her room. When Susannah woke in the morning, she would read what Phillis had written the night before.

Susannah had known from the first day she met her that Phillis was bright. But now Susannah had discovered that Phillis had a gift that she should share with the world. That gift was poetry.

PARADISE LOST.

BOOK I.

OF Mans First Disobedience, and the Fruit
Of that Forbidden Tree, whose mortal tast
Brought Death into the World, and all our woe,
With loss of Eden, till one greater Man
Restore us, and regain the blissful Seat,
Sing Heav'nly Muse, that on the secret top
Of *Oreb*, or of *Sinai*, didst inspire
That Shepherd, who first taught the chosen Seed,
In the Beginning how the Heav'ns and Earth
Rose out of *Chaos* : Or if *Sion* Hill
Delight thee more, and *Siloa's* Brook that flow'd
Fast by the Oracle of God ; I thence
Invoke thy aid to my adventrous Song,
That with no middle flight intends to soar
A   Above

This is a photo of a page from *Paradise Lost* by John Milton, which was printed in 1667.

Fame in Boston

Susannah was proud of Phillis. She wanted to show off Phillis's talents. Susannah began to invite important people in Boston to the Wheatley home so that they could hear Phillis read her poetry. The rich families of Boston enjoyed the young girl's poetry because it was about all the important things in their own lives. Phillis's poems were about things like religion and how to be a good person.

Phillis got to meet very important people because of her poetry. She met the **governor** and **lieutenant governor** of Massachusetts, Thomas Hutchinson and Andrew Oliver. She also met John Hancock, whose signature was the largest one on the **Declaration of Independence.**

Thomas Hutchinson served as Great Britain's governor of Massachusetts from 1771 to 1774.

This picture shows a slave serving a meal in a home in the **colony** of New York.

Susannah sent Phillis to read her poetry in Boston's finest houses. She wanted everyone to know this talented girl. Phillis was special to Susannah, but some people looked only at Phillis's skin and didn't care about her talent.

Those people were uncomfortable having a **slave** in their home. They thought slaves were supposed to prepare and serve meals and clean, not read poetry to them. However, most families welcomed Phillis into their homes and enjoyed her poetry.

A Published Poet

Susannah wanted more than just the people of Boston to experience Phillis's poetry. She wanted all of the **colonies** to have that chance. Susannah wanted Phillis's poems to be collected in a book. Books were valuable to people then because they were expensive and hard to get.

Susannah was able to find a printer in Great Britain to **publish** Phillis's poems in a book. Archibald Bell said he would print the book, but he wanted proof that Phillis was really a **slave.**

This machine was used to print words on paper. It was brought to the colonies in 1640.

> But still you cry: "O Charles! thy manly mind,
> "Enwrap our souls, and all thy actions bind:
> "Our only hope, more dear than vital breath,
> "Twelve moons revolv'd, and sunk in shades of death!
> "Engaging infant! Nightly visions give
> "Thee to our arms, and we with joy recieve;
> "We fain would clasp the Phantom to our breast,
> "The Phantom flies, and leaves the soul unblest!"
> Prepare to meet your dearest infant friend
> Where joys are pure, and glory's without end.
>
> Boston, Sept.r 1st 1772.   Phillis Wheatley.

Phyllis's handwriting can be seen in this poem she wrote in 1772. Her signature is in the right lower corner.

Susannah collected the signatures of eighteen famous and powerful men who lived in Boston. The men signed their names on a document that said Phillis was a slave. It also said that she wrote the poetry that was to be printed in the book. Thomas Hutchinson, Andrew Oliver, John Hancock, and John Wheatley were some of the men who signed the document.

The signatures convinced Bell, and he agreed to publish the book. In the spring of 1773, Phillis sailed to Great Britain. Susannah wanted Phillis to be famous there, too.

Great Britain and Freedom

Phillis went to Great Britain with Nathaniel Wheatley, who was about to be married to a girl who lived there. Phillis's first journey on a ship made her a **slave,** but her second trip would make her a free woman.

Although the colonies of America belonged to Great Britain, slavery was not allowed there. A new British law stated that any slave visiting Great Britain would be freed. At the age of 20, Phillis was no longer a slave.

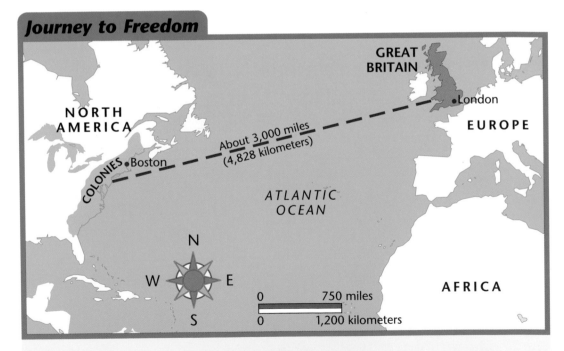

Journey to Freedom

GREAT BRITAIN

London

NORTH AMERICA

EUROPE

About 3,000 miles
(4,828 kilometers)

COLONIES • Boston

ATLANTIC OCEAN

N
W   E
S

AFRICA

0   750 miles
0   1,200 kilometers

In 1750, about 700,000 people lived in the city of London. This map shows how far Phillis had to sail.

This historic drawing shows the River Thames and the city of London.

Just like she did in Boston, Phillis met many important people in Great Britain. People wanted to meet the slave who wrote poetry. The King and Queen of England were away from London for the summer. Otherwise, Phillis would have met King George III, the most powerful man in the world at that time. Just before her book, *Poems on Various Subjects, Religious and Moral,* was to be printed, Phillis received a letter that said Susannah was very sick. Phillis sailed back to Boston right away.

Phillis's Poem

In a poem called "On the Death of a young Lady of Five Years of Age," Phillis tried to comfort the parents of a child who had died. She wrote that they would see their child in heaven. These are the last two lines of the poem:

Yourselves, safe landed on the blissful shore,
Shall join your happy babe to part no more.

Books, Sadness, and War

Phillis returned to Boston a free woman, but she went right back to the Wheatley house to take care of Susannah, who was very sick. She also waited for copies of her book to arrive from London. Phillis was supposed to receive 300 copies of the book. It took months for her books to arrive in Boston.

The book was printed in September 1773. It was so popular in Great Britain that Bell sold all the books quickly. Phillis finally received her books in the spring of 1774. Now that she was a free woman, Phillis needed to sell her copies of the books to make money to take care of herself. Phillis put ads in Boston newspapers and sold all the copies of her book.

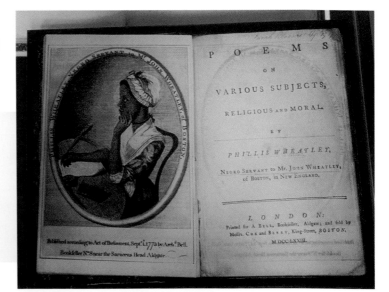

This is a copy of Wheatley's book that is on display at the Old South Meeting House in Boston.

One of the first battles of the Revolutionary War broke out at Lexington, Massachusetts, on April 19, 1775.

On March 3, 1774, Susannah Wheatley died. She was 65 years old. Phillis lost the person who took care of her the most in her life.

From 1775–1783, soldiers from the **colonies** fought a war with Great Britain because the colonies wanted to be a separate country. The war was called the **Revolutionary War.** The first battles of the war were fought in Lexington and Concord, just outside of Boston. Phillis believed that the colonies should be free, but the Wheatleys believed that Great Britain should still rule the colonies.

Meeting George Washington

Phillis wanted to honor the man chosen to lead the armies of the **colonies,** General George Washington. She wrote a poem about the general from Virginia and sent it to him early in 1776. The poem was lost in Washington's office papers.

In 1776, George Washington, above, wrote a thank-you letter to Phillis. In the letter, he said Phillis had "great poetical talents."

When Washington finally found the poem a few months later, he loved it. He sent a letter to Phillis inviting her to visit his headquarters in Cambridge, Massachusetts. Phillis made plans immediately to visit George Washington. Cambridge was only a **carriage** ride away.

This house in Cambridge, Massachusetts, once served as Washington's headquarters.

Washington owned many **slaves** that worked on his **plantation** in Virginia. It was very unusual for a slave owner from the South to visit with a slave or former slave. But Washington spent half an hour talking with Phillis at his headquarters in March 1776. There is no record of what the two talked about. But Washington told others that he thought Phillis was a genius, or a very smart person.

Poor and Forgotten

Early in 1778, John Wheatley died. Shortly after that, his daughter, Mary, died too. Nathaniel Wheatley died in 1783. The Wheatleys, including Susannah, didn't leave Phillis any money in their **wills.** Phillis was free, but that also meant that she had to take care of herself.

Phillis thought the best way to make money was to sell more of her poetry. She placed ads in the Boston newspapers to try to find buyers for a new book she would **publish.**

During and after the war, people could not afford to buy books. This is a page from a book published in 1778.

The **Revolutionary War** had made life hard for the people of America. People didn't have as much money as they did before the war. What little money the people of Boston did have was spent on food, clothing, and places to live. The people who loved books just didn't have the money to buy them.

Phillis didn't find the money to print another book of her poetry, but she did find love. In the spring of 1778, she married John Peters.

The Revolutionary War was still going on when Phillis got married. The Battle of Monmouth, shown above, was fought on June 28, 1778.

Alone Again

John Peters was a former slave who had many talents. At different times in his life, he was a lawyer, barber, grocer, baker, and a doctor. John and Phillis lived in a big, nice house in Boston on Queen Street, which is called Court Street today. A year after they were married, Phillis gave birth to a baby, but the baby died. John and Phillis had another baby a few years later, but that baby also died.

Baby Names

No one knows the names of Phillis's babies. Phillis might have written poetry about her babies, but if she did, the poetry has been lost.

This is what Court Street in Boston looks like today.

The prison that John had to go to probably looked a lot like this one, shown in a drawing from 1809.

John had money problems and lost his grocery store. In 1784, he went to prison because he owed other people money and he couldn't pay them. Phillis was forced to move to a home for the poor.

Phillis had another baby in the fall of 1784. She had to do hard, physical work in the home to buy food for her baby. Phillis became very sick. On December 5, 1784, she died. A few hours later, so did her baby. Nobody came to her funeral, except a minister, and no one knows where she is buried.

An Amazing Woman

Many people think that Phillis Wheatley was an amazing woman. Some people never get over bad things that happen in their lives. But Phillis recovered from being stolen from her family in Africa and being made a **slave.** She became a famous poet as well.

Phillis came to a new land not knowing a single word of English. She not only learned the language of her new home, but she was also able to use it to make thoughtful, beautiful poetry.

This rare picture of Wheatley shows her wearing a dress and jewelry. It was featured in a journal in Paris, France, sometime between 1834 and 1842.

It would have been easy for Phillis to just give up and accept what life seemed to have planned for her. But she didn't. The world was not always kind to Phillis, but she was still able to find things she loved about life and write about them.

Historians remember Phillis as more than just a slave who wrote poetry. She is remembered as the first African-American poet and as a poet whose writing helped people see the good things in their lives.

This statue of Phillis was made in 1973 by a woman named Elizabeth Catlett. It is in an art museum in Cincinnati, Ohio.

Glossary

astronomy study of the stars and planets

auction sale of property to a person who offers to pay the most for it

carriage four-wheeled vehicle pulled by horses and used for carrying people

colony group of people who move to another land but are still ruled by the same country they moved from. People who live in a colony are called colonists.

Declaration of Independence document that said the United States was an independent nation. Independent means not under the control or rule of another person or government.

geography study of places in the world and the plants, animals, and weather of those places

governor person who is elected to lead a state. In colonial times, a governor helped lead a colony.

lieutenant governor person who helps the governor lead a state, or colony in colonial times

mythology study of the stories of groups in history whose stories have been handed down and remembered

plantation large farm on which one main crop is grown by workers who live there

publish make available for sale a book or other printed work

Revolutionary War war from 1775 to 1783 in which the American colonists won freedom from Great Britain

slave person who is owned by another person

tutor teacher who teaches one student at a time

will legal paper that tells what should be done with a person's property and money after that person dies

More Books to Read

Greene, Carol. *Phillis Wheatley: First African American Poet*. Danbury, Conn.: Scholastic Library Publishing, 2000.

Gregson, Susan R. *Phillis Wheatley*. Mankato, Minn.: Capstone Press, 2002.

Salisbury, Cynthia. *Phillis Wheatley: Legendary African-American Poet*. Berkeley Heights, N.J.: Enslow Publishers, 2001.

Places to Visit

Old South Meeting House

310 Washington Street

Boston, Massachusetts 02108

Visitor Information: (617) 482-6439

City of Boston

Greater Boston Convention & Visitors Bureau

Two Copley Place, Suite 105

Boston, Massachusetts 02116

Visitor Information: (888) 733-BOSTON

Index

Africa 6, 28

astronomy 12

Atlantic Ocean 4

Bell, Archibald 16, 17, 20

Boston, Massachusetts 6, 7, 14, 15, 16, 17, 20, 25

Cambridge, Massachusetts 22

Catlett, Elizabeth 29

Cincinnati, Ohio 29

Concord, Massachusetts 21

Declaration of Independence 14

Fitch, Timothy 6

geography 12

George III, King 19

Great Britain 16, 17, 18, 19, 20, 21

Hancock, John 14, 17

harbor of Boston 6

history 12

Hutchinson, Thomas 14, 17

King Street 8

Lexington, Massachusetts 21

London, England 6, 19, 20

Milton, John 13

mythology 12

Old South Meeting House 11, 20

Oliver, Andrew 14, 17

Peters, John 7, 25, 26, 27

Phillis (ship) 6

Poems on Various Subjects, Religious and Moral 19, 20

poetry 6, 12–13, 14, 15, 16, 17, 19, 22, 24, 25, 26, 28, 29

Revolutionary War 21, 25

slave traders 6

Washington, George 7, 22–23

Wheatley, John 8, 17, 24

Wheatley, Mary 9, 11, 24

Wheatley, Nathaniel 11, 18, 24

Wheatley, Susannah 7, 8, 11, 13, 14, 15, 16, 17, 19, 20, 21, 24